Sister,
I Want to Know
Your Story

This book is for

_____

Introduction

The purpose of this book to share more of yourself with your beloved brothers and sisters. By sharing your life story, thoughts and memories, they will be able to know you in an entirely new way. They'll discover the important details and moments that formed the foundation of your life, and also the little things that helped you to become the person they know and love today.

This book will become a cherished family heirloom that will be passed down to future generations to teach them about their family's history, roots and values.

The book is divided into sections, beginning with your early childhood memories and details. Each section features writing prompts for you to answer, followed by several pages for you to record other memories, thoughts and life lessons learned that you would like to share. Take your time in filling out the answers: there are no right or wrong responses.

The gift of your story and accumulated wisdom is one that your family will cherish in the years to come!

Table of Contents

Roots:
My Family Tree

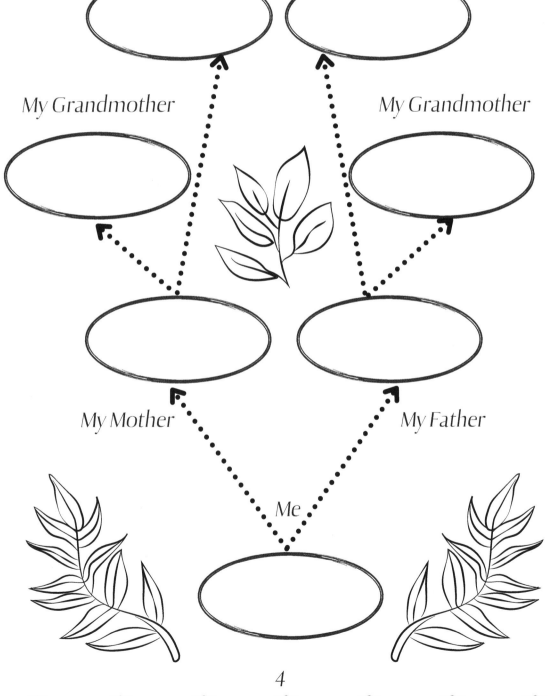

My Grandfather

My Grandfather

My Grandmother

My Grandmother

My Mother

My Father

Me

In the beginning:
Childhood Memories

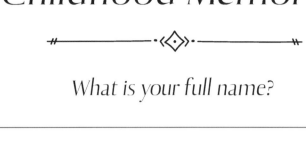

In the beginning:
Childhood Memories

What is your full name?

_____

Were you named after someone, or does your name have
any special meaning or significance?

_____
_____
_____

What was your date of birth and where were you born?

_____
_____
_____

How old were your parents when you were born?

_____
_____

Do you know what size you were at birth?

_____
_____

Did you have any nicknames?

_____

How many siblings did you have? Were they older or younger than you? What are their names?

_____
_____
_____
_____

Did your parents share any special stories about you as a baby or very young child?

_____
_____
_____
_____
_____
_____
_____
_____
_____
_____
_____
_____
_____
_____
_____
_____
_____
_____
_____

What is your earliest memory?

_____
_____
_____
_____

Did you have any serious childhood accidents or illnesses?

_____
_____
_____

What were your parents' names, when were they born and where did they grow up?

_____
_____
_____

Describe any special memories of your mother and what she was like when you were little.

_____
_____
_____
_____
_____
_____
_____
_____

Describe any special memories of your father and what he was like when you were little.

_____
_____
_____
_____
_____
_____
_____
_____
_____
_____

Describe any special memories of your grandparents or other close family members when you were little.

_____
_____
_____
_____
_____
_____
_____
_____
_____
_____
_____
_____
_____

What was your favorite holiday growing up?

_____

_____

Were there any family traditions that made it special?

_____

_____

_____

_____

Did you have birthday parties? What were they like?

_____

_____

_____

_____

_____

What family vacations stand out in your memory?

_____

_____

_____

_____

_____

_____

_____

_____

_____

What did you want to be when you grew up?

_____

_____

What were your childhood home and neighborhood like?

_____

_____

_____

_____

Were you afraid of anything as a child, such as the dark or spiders?

_____

_____

_____

Did you believe in Santa Claus, the Easter Bunny, the Tooth Fairy, etc? What were your family traditions?

_____

_____

_____

_____

_____

_____

_____

_____

_____

Childhood Memories

Childhood Memories

_____

_____

_____

_____

_____

_____

_____

_____

_____

_____

_____

_____

_____

_____

_____

_____

_____

_____

_____

_____

_____

_____

_____

_____

_____

_____

_____

_____

_____

_____

Childhood Memories

_____
_____
_____
_____
_____
_____
_____
_____
_____
_____
_____
_____
_____
_____
_____
_____
_____
_____
_____
_____
_____
_____
_____
_____
_____

Childhood Memories

_____
_____
_____
_____
_____
_____
_____
_____
_____
_____
_____
_____
_____
_____
_____
_____
_____
_____
_____
_____
_____
_____
_____
_____
_____
_____
_____
_____
_____

Childhood Memories

Growing up:
Adolescence

Growing up:
Adolescence

—— ·◇· ——

What schools did you attend growing up? Where were they?

_____
_____
_____
_____

Did you like school? What were your favorite and least favorite subjects?

_____
_____
_____
_____

What school clubs and activities were you involved in?

_____
_____
_____
_____
_____
_____
_____
_____
_____
_____

What activities were you involved in outside of school?

_____

_____

_____

_____

Did you participate in any sports?

_____

_____

_____

_____

Did you learn to play a musical instrument?

_____

_____

How were your grades?

_____

_____

Do you have any special memories of attending Prom,
Homecoming, etc.?

_____

_____

_____

_____

_____

Who were your friends and what did you like to do together?

_____

_____

_____

_____

How old were you when you learned to drive and who taught
you? Did you have a car?

_____

_____

_____

Were you allowed to date? At what age? Who was your first
date with and what did you do?

_____

_____

_____

_____

_____

What type of clothing did you like to wear in high school?
Was your hair long or short?

_____

_____

_____

_____

_____

_____

What type of music did you listen to and who were your favorite artists? Favorite song?

_____

_____

_____

_____

How was your relationship with your parents during those years?

_____

_____

_____

_____

Did you go on any special trips with your family or school?

_____

_____

_____

_____

Did you have a graduation celebration?

_____

_____

_____

_____

_____

_____

_____

Adolescent Memories

Adolescent Memories

Adolescent Memories

_____
_____
_____
_____
_____
_____
_____
_____
_____
_____
_____
_____
_____
_____
_____
_____
_____
_____
_____
_____
_____
_____
_____
_____
_____
_____
_____
_____
_____

Adolescent Memories

_____

_____

_____

_____

_____

_____

_____

_____

_____

_____

_____

_____

_____

_____

_____

_____

_____

_____

_____

_____

_____

_____

_____

_____

_____

_____

_____

_____

_____

Adolescent Memories

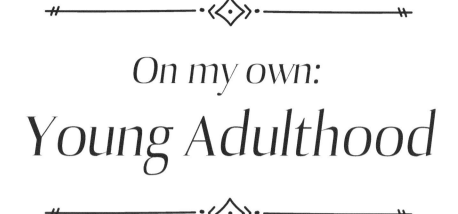

On my own:
Young Adulthood

On my own:
Young Adulthood

--- ·«◇»· ---

Did you attend school after high school? If not, why not?

_____

_____

_____

If so, where did your attend college and what did you major in? Did you graduate?

_____

_____

_____

Where did you live while in college?

_____

_____

_____

Which of the things you learned in school has been the most helpful to you in the real world?

_____

_____

_____

_____

_____

What organized activities were you involved in during college?

_____

_____

_____

_____

How did you and your friends spend your spare time?

_____

_____

_____

_____

Did you study abroad? If so, where and what did you like the most about the experience?

_____

_____

_____

_____

_____

_____

How long did it take to find your first job after graduating? What was it?

_____

_____

_____

_____

_____

Did you serve in the military? If so, for how long? Which branch? What rank did you achieve and what was your job?

_____
_____
_____
_____
_____
_____

Where were you stationed or deployed?

_____
_____
_____

Did you see combat?

_____
_____

How did your military service change you?

_____
_____
_____
_____
_____
_____
_____
_____

Where did you live after leaving home and who did you live with?

_____

_____

_____

Have you ever experienced "love at first sight" and did it work out?

_____

_____

_____

_____

What was the most romantic date you remember ever going on?

_____

_____

_____

_____

_____

What was the worst date you remember?

_____

_____

_____

_____

_____

_____

Young Adult Memories

Young Adult Memories

Young Adult Memories

Young Adult Memories

Young Adult Memories

Starting a family:
Marriage & Children

TELL ME
YOUR
STORY

Starting a family:
Marriage & Children

——— ·«◇»· ———

How did you meet your husband?

_____
_____
_____
_____
_____

What qualities attracted you to him?

_____
_____
_____
_____

What did you do on your first date together?

_____
_____
_____
_____
_____
_____
_____

How long did you date before you got engaged? How long were you engaged before you got married?

_____

_____

_____

How did he propose?

_____

_____

_____

_____

When and where did you get married?

_____

_____

What do you remember most about your wedding?

_____

_____

_____

_____

_____

_____

Did you go on a honeymoon? Where did you go?

_____

_____

_____

Where was your first home together and what was it like?

_____
_____
_____
_____
_____

Where did you each work?

_____
_____
_____
_____

What did you do for fun as a couple in the early years?

_____
_____
_____
_____
_____

What was the hardest thing to adjust to about being married?

_____
_____
_____
_____
_____

How did you divide the household chores?

_____

_____

_____

How did you celebrate your first anniversary?

_____

_____

_____

_____

Did you take any special trips together?

_____

_____

_____

_____

What do you love most about your husband?

_____

_____

_____

What does he do that drives you crazy?

_____

_____

_____

How long were you married before your first child arrived?

_____

_____

How did it feel, knowing that you were about to become a mother?

_____

_____

_____

_____

What are your children's names and birthdates?

_____

_____

_____

_____

_____

How did becoming a mother change your life?

_____

_____

_____

_____

_____

_____

_____

_____

Did you get to watch your children being born?

_____
_____
_____

Did you raise your children in the same way that your parents raised you, or did you do things differently?

_____
_____
_____
_____

How old were you when I was born?

_____
_____

What special memories do you have of me as a child?

_____
_____
_____
_____
_____
_____
_____
_____
_____

What do you love best about me?

_____

_____

_____

_____

What makes you proudest as a sister?

_____

_____

_____

_____

_____

What are your favorite traditions within our family?

_____

_____

_____

_____

_____

What was your favorite family trip while your children were growing up?

_____

_____

_____

_____

_____

What are some special family times that you remember of us?

_____
_____
_____
_____
_____
_____
_____
_____
_____
_____
_____
_____
_____
_____
_____
_____
_____

Is there anything you wish you had done differently as a sister?

_____
_____
_____
_____
_____
_____
_____
_____

Family Memories

Family Memories

Family Memories

Family Memories

Family Memories

The working years:
Earning a Living

The working years:

Earning a Living

—◈—

What was your first job?

_____

_____

_____

_____

What jobs have you held during your life?

_____

_____

_____

_____

_____

_____

_____

What is your profession?

_____

_____

_____

_____

_____

_____

How did you learn to do your job?

_____

_____

_____

_____

What is the best job you ever had? What did you most like about it?

_____

_____

_____

_____

_____

_____

_____

_____

_____

What was your least favorite job? Why?

_____

_____

_____

_____

_____

_____

_____

_____

Which job was the most fun?

_____
_____
_____
_____

Did your career turn out as you expected?

_____
_____
_____
_____
_____
_____
_____

Is there a job you would like to have held, but never had the opportunity?

_____
_____
_____
_____

Who was your favorite boss and why?

_____
_____
_____
_____
_____

What did you dislike the most about having to go to work each day?

_____

_____

_____

_____

Did your work give you a sense of fulfillment?

_____

_____

_____

_____

_____

_____

_____

_____

What are you looking forward to in retirement?

_____

_____

_____

_____

_____

_____

_____

_____

_____

Work Memories

Work Memories

Work Memories

Work Memories

Work Memories

Time goes on:
Getting Older

Time goes on:
Getting Older

─◈─

What places are still on your bucket list to visit?

_____
_____
_____
_____
_____

What things are on your bucket list yet to try doing?

_____
_____
_____
_____
_____

How have your priorities changed as you've gotten older?

_____
_____
_____
_____
_____
_____
_____

Do you have any health challenges?

_____
_____
_____
_____
_____

Of what accomplishment are you most proud so far?

_____
_____
_____
_____
_____
_____
_____
_____

Is there anything you would change about your life if you could?

_____
_____
_____
_____
_____
_____
_____

What are you most thankful for in your life?

_____
_____
_____
_____
_____

If you could say anything to your younger self, what would it be?

_____
_____
_____
_____
_____

Is there anything you wish you had known sooner?

_____
_____
_____
_____
_____

Who has had the biggest influence on your life?

_____
_____
_____
_____
_____

If you could revisit any period in your life, when would it be and why?

_____
_____
_____
_____
_____
_____
_____

What events in your life do you feel helped make you who you are today?

_____
_____
_____
_____
_____
_____
_____

What would you like your legacy to be?

_____
_____
_____
_____
_____
_____
_____

How many grandchildren do you have? What are their names and when were they born?

_____
_____
_____
_____
_____
_____
_____

How did your life change when you became a grandparent?

_____
_____
_____
_____
_____
_____
_____

How are you different with your grandchildren than you were with your own children?

_____
_____
_____
_____
_____
_____
_____

What do you love the most about being a grandparent?

_____
_____
_____
_____
_____
_____
_____

What hopes do you have for your grandchildren?

_____
_____
_____
_____
_____
_____
_____

Do you have any great-grandchildren? What are their names and when were they born?

_____
_____
_____
_____
_____
_____
_____
_____

Later Memories

Later Memories

Later Memories

Later Memories

Later Memories

More about me:
My Values & Beliefs

TELL ME
YOUR
STORY

More about me:
My Values & Beliefs

—·◈·—

Do you believe in God?

_____

_____

_____

_____

_____

Do you pray, and if so, how often?

_____

_____

_____

_____

Are you a member of an organized religion? If so, which one?

_____

_____

_____

_____

Do you attend regular religious services or meetings?

_____

_____

_____

Do you belong to a political party? Which one?

_____

_____

Do you vote?

_____

_____

Have you ever been the victim of prejudice for any reason?

_____

_____

_____

_____

_____

_____

_____

What do you think can be done to overcome prejudice?

_____

_____

_____

_____

_____

Were you taught any personal prejudices as a child?

_____

_____

_____

What values do you feel are most important?

_____
_____
_____
_____
_____

Have you been able to incorporate these values into your family?

_____
_____
_____
_____
_____

What changes would you like to see in the world to make it a better place?

_____
_____
_____
_____
_____
_____
_____
_____
_____
_____
_____

More about me:
My Interests & Favorites

Do you have any hobbies? Why do you enjoy them?

_____
_____
_____
_____
_____

What other hobbies have you tried? Why did you stop doing them?

_____
_____
_____
_____
_____

Do you collect anything?

_____
_____
_____

What was your first car? What is your favorite car?

_____
_____

Do you enjoy traveling? Do you have a passport?

_____

_____

What countries have you visited and which was your favorite?

_____

_____

_____

_____

_____

_____

What languages do you speak?

_____

_____

_____

How many states have you visited? Which do you like best?

_____

_____

_____

_____

_____

_____

What is your favorite city to visit?

_____

_____

Would you rather fly or drive?

_____

Where is your favorite vacation spot?

_____

What is your favorite way to spend a weekend?

_____
_____
_____
_____

What is your favorite way to relax?

_____
_____
_____
_____

How would you describe your perfect day?

_____
_____
_____
_____
_____
_____
_____
_____

What sports have you played?

_____
_____
_____

Which sports do you like to watch?

_____
_____
_____

What are your favorite teams?

_____
_____
_____

Do you play a musical instrument? If so, which one?

_____

What is your favorite type of music to listen to?

_____
_____

Do you have a favorite song?

_____

What was your favorite concert you've attended?

_____
_____

What do you do for exercise? Do you enjoy it?

_____

_____

Do you have a favorite museum?

_____

What is your favorite board game or card game?

_____

_____

What would you like to try doing, but haven't yet?

_____

_____

_____

_____

What genres do you enjoy reading?

_____

_____

_____

What is your favorite book? Who is your favorite author?

_____

_____

Do you prefer actual books, electronic books or audio books?

_____

Do you play video or any other electronic games?

_____

_____

What is your favorite TV show? What do you like about it?

_____

_____

_____

What is your favorite movie?

_____

_____

Have you ever been to a drive-in movie?

_____

Who are your favorite actor and actress?

_____

_____

Who would you most like to have a conversation with if you could, living or dead?

_____

What would you ask them?

_____

_____

_____

How do you like to spend your free time?

_____

_____

_____

What do you think your talents are?

_____

_____

What do other people think you're good at?

_____

_____

What is your favorite animal?

_____

What pets have you had during your lifetime?

_____

_____

_____

_____

If your parents have passed away, when did they die and what was the cause?

_____

_____

_____

_____

Are you a "morning person" or a "night owl?"

_____
_____

What are your favorite foods?

_____
_____
_____

What is your favorite restaurant and what do you like to order there?

_____
_____

What is your favorite dessert? Do you have a "sweet tooth?"

_____
_____

What are your favorite beverages -- hot, cold and cocktail?

_____
_____
_____

Do you have any superstitions?

_____
_____
_____
_____

Do you believe in astrology? What is your zodiac sign?

_____

_____

How many times have you been married?

_____

_____

What is your favorite color?

_____

What is your favorite day of the week?

_____

Do you like to gamble or buy lottery tickets?

_____

_____

_____

What is your favorite flower?

_____

Do you have a favorite type of weather? What is your favorite season?

_____

_____

_____

_____

Do you have a "lucky number?"

_____

What kind of candy do you like best?

_____

What is your favorite smell?

_____

Do you have a favorite flower?

_____

Do you enjoy cooking or baking? What is your specialty?

_____

_____

_____

Do you have a favorite quote?

_____

_____

_____

_____

What is your favorite holiday?

_____

_____

_____

_____

Other Memories to Share

Other Memories to Share

Other Memories to Share

Other Memories to Share

Other Memories to Share

Other Memories to Share

Other Memories to Share

Other Memories to Share

Other Memories to Share

Other Memories to Share

Other Memories to Share

_____
_____
_____
_____
_____
_____
_____
_____
_____
_____
_____
_____
_____
_____
_____
_____
_____
_____
_____
_____
_____
_____
_____
_____
_____
_____
_____
_____

Other Memories to Share

Other Memories to Share

Final Thoughts

633678d-42d5-4490-8e7d-e4b435695529R01

Made in the USA
Monee, IL
24 October 2024